Measuring your IT
Identifying the metrics that matter

D0880039

Measuring your IT

Identifying the metrics that matter

JOHN STEWART

IT Governance Publishing

IT Governance Publishing
IT Governance Limited
Unit 3, Clive Court
Bartholomew's Walk
Cambridgeshire Business Park
Ely
Cambridgeshire
CB7 4EA
United Kingdom

www.itgovernance.co.uk

© John Stewart 2012
The author has asserted the rights of the author under the Copyright, Designs and Patents Act, 1988, to be identified as the author of this work.

First published in the United Kingdom in 2012
by IT Governance Publishing.

ISBN 978-1-84928-436-3

PREFACE

Measurement: preaching to the converted?

Be honest: hands up. Who thinks measurement is boring? It doesn't exactly give you a sense of well-being or peace or joy or love: it doesn't rate very highly as a contributor to quality of life. I hope those of you with a mathematical bent won't be offended.

You may only be reading this because your boss told you to, or because your boss gave you responsibility for sorting out some metrics. Maybe your bonus depends on how well you do against metrics, so you want to use them to show your work in a good light. Maybe you've been told you need metrics to be able to manage your own work.

But wait a minute. If you need convincing of the case for effective measurement, here are some things to think about.

Measurement is better than our own subjective judgements in letting us know how good or bad things are. As I write, parts of the UK have just had weeks of wet weather; a year ago we had a drought. So was the rain normal or unprecedented?

Measurement guides us as to how good things could be; based on previous summers' measurements, if you live in Cannes you can reasonably look forward to 10 hours' sunshine a day, which is a kind of target, though not a good one, as we can't control it.

Measurement provides objectivity: you might find 25 degrees Celsius pleasantly warm; to me it's too hot. With a number, we can't argue about how hot it is; we can still argue of course about whether we like it!

Measurement lets us compare. Are the days getting warmer? Is it better where you are than where your sister is?

Measurement provides us with a common truth. Not only do you know you're only doing 70 miles an hour, so do the police.

What has all this got to do with IT? Quite a lot, actually, as we shall see.

ABOUT THE AUTHOR

After graduating from Glasgow University with a 1st class honours degree in Chemistry, John Stewart worked for 38 years as a public servant. He spent five years as an IT adviser in London and Newcastle universities. He then joined the Central Computer and Telecommunications Agency (CCTA), the UK government's IT agency, where he founded and led the early development of ITIL®, now a global success, and instigated the development of PRINCE2®. He became responsible for all CCTA's IT-related best practice and successfully transformed the organisation to cover its costs by charging for its services. John held a number of senior positions in the Office of Government Commerce (OGC). He instigated the drive to buy common goods and services centrally to get better value for money. Latterly he was Director of Procurement Policy, where his responsibilities included efforts to get more SMEs into government supply chains. He is now undertaking freelance work, including Programme Director at the International Best Practice Institute (IBPI).

ACKNOWLEDGEMENTS

I'm grateful to all at IT Governance Group for their support, encouragement and forbearance. My thanks to Brian Johnson, CA Technologies, long-time friend and colleague for introducing me to ITG, for helping me get to grips with working life after decades in the civil service and for very helpful content suggestions. Thank you also to my other reviewers, Chris Evans, ITSM Specialist and Dave Jones, Pink Elephant for their helpful suggestions and comments.

Thanks to Ivo van Haren for agreeing to me working for a competitor while I'm working with him at the IBPI. Thanks too to the many friends, colleagues and critics who have worked with me on IT matters over the years, who have helped shape my experience and from whom I've learned a great deal.

I'm really grateful to my daughter, Caroline, for her work preparing the graphs and diagrams. However, most of all, thanks to my wife, Anne, for her patience while I've disappeared for hours and days preparing my thoughts and putting finger to keyboard.

CONTENTS

Contents

INTRODUCTION

What this book is about

The book is intended as an introduction to measurement – why it's important, who's involved and the sorts of things that you may want or need to measure. It should give you enough to whet your appetite to dig deeper, if you need to.

If you're a business user, the book aims to help you to get the best out of your IT. If you're an IT provider, it should help you to give your customers the best value for money.

It should help you answer the questions: is our IT good enough? How does it compare now with last quarter, last year? How is ours compared with others', be they friends, rivals or competitors?

What this book isn't

As the book is intended to provide an overview of the why and what of IT measurement, it isn't an encyclopaedia on the subject. There are many other books available that provide in-depth coverage.

Who should read the book?

The book is intended for anyone who is interested in understanding IT measurement better. The book is meant to foster an understanding between business managers and users who depend on IT, on the one hand, and IT providers on the other hand, so should be appealing to both.

CHAPTER 1: IT MEASUREMENT IN CONTEXT

I think therefore I am. I measure therefore I act. Anonymous.

Why measure IT

Quite simply, if you want to understand, control or improve your IT, or communicate it to others, you need measurement.

If you want to know how good your IT is, both in terms of quality and value for money, you need to measure it. Then you'll understand whether you can keep it as it is, or need to do something about it. Or at least you will, if you know what measurement ranges constitute good and not so good practice.

If you want to know if your IT is heading in the right direction, or is set to give you a nasty shock or a disappointed, sinking feeling, you need to find things to measure that will tell you so. That way, you'll know whether you can relax or, on the other hand, need to take action.

It's a bit like a car driver and the speedometer: too fast and you need to brake, too slow and you need to accelerate. Like the speedometer, IT measures are context-specific. What is 'in the right ballpark' on a dual carriageway may be quite inappropriate for a winding country lane; IT performance as measured in a large steady state operation may be hugely over-ambitious for a not-yet-stable new operation.

Client perspectives

The key stakeholders on the client side will want measures that show if they are getting what they need and what they are paying for. If not, remedial action will be needed.

Let's start with who pays: the business overseen by the Board. It doesn't matter if it has in-house IT or if it is externally sourced. At the very least, it'll want to:

- know it's getting what it's asked for;
- check what it's asked for works for the business and its users;
- be satisfied it's getting value for money;
- know things not working for it are fixed quickly in line with the needs of the business and to know necessary changes are managed through effectively.

To give it the governance it needs requires measurement.

The users, whose work may be completely dependent on IT, will want to:

- have a service that is 'just there', working reliably and as required;
- have problems dealt with quickly and efficiently;
- feel the provider is responsive and communicative;
- have their say on what is and isn't good about the service – and to be confident something will be done about their feedback.

Provider perspectives

It's a pretty good idea for the IT provider to understand and work to the business's success criteria for its IT. If the IT provider is serving a lot of businesses it still needs to have measures that align with how these businesses judge their IT as successfully supporting them.

The IT provider will need much more, though. Here is a selection of essentials, which, however, will not be sufficient for every provider's needs:

- Are we complying with the contractual or agreed terms?
- What do the users think? Do they have niggles with our performance (which we need to address)?
- How is our productivity? How do our unit costs compare with others'? (If we're lagging our competitiveness is at risk.)
- How good is our problem and change management performance?
- Do our projects deliver to spec, time and budget? If not do we know why and do we know what to do to put things right?

Contracts and agreements

What the client expects of the provider is normally set out in a contract or service level agreement (SLA). Measurement is used to assess and demonstrate achievement of the required terms of the contract or agreement.

Providers should aim to comply with SLAs. Applied 'within the family', they are used as a basis for assessing how things are going and for deciding what and how to improve.

Contracts mean more than that. They apply when the client and provider are in different organisations, albeit sometimes with the same parent organisation. Failure to comply with a contract will have consequences, possibly of a financial nature, so a lot of effort is usually deployed to stay on the right side of compliance!

How often should you measure IT?

Operational services like IT need to be continually managed and that means measurement, otherwise there is an ever-present danger of them falling into disrepair. Measurement provides an objective basis for management action.

Some things need daily attention, some even hourly or by-the-minute. A business-critical incident may need continual management attention, aided by measurements and assessments, just as, for example, a skid needs to be managed from start to hopefully accident-free end, with the aid of the speedometer, the steering wheel and eyes looking out the window.

Other things will need to be re-assessed less frequently, but, nevertheless, regularly. Thus, although a problem causing the service to be unavailable will have to be addressed there and then, a longer-term perspective on availability is needed to make sure required service levels are met and to enable weaknesses to be addressed. So, service availability may be measured on 13 consecutive periods, each of 4 weeks, over the course of the year, or on rolling, overlapping periods, e.g. 13 weeks (quarter of a year) rolled forward every 4 weeks.

Thus, frequency depends on what you're measuring and why. Frequency, like the measures themselves, is context-specific.

Who should measure? For whom?

Everybody is responsible so nobody is responsible. Anonymous.

The IT provider will invariably be responsible for giving the client business the bulk of measurements it requires about its IT, though it may choose to do spot checks itself and to arrange for its own customer satisfaction surveys to be carried out.

The IT provider's senior management will need measurements from the teams responsible for particular aspects of the service or from nominated individuals with specific responsibility for obtaining and reporting on the information needed. For example, the service desk manager might be responsible for reporting on incident-handling performance; alternatively, a single manager could be responsible for both incident and problem management, and so be charged with reporting on both.

What do you do with the measurements?

The question is unknown, but the answer is 42: loosely taken from *The Hitchhiker's Guide to the Galaxy* (Douglas Adams, 1979).

When you measure, it's a good idea if you know what to do with the measurement. If your speedometer says 35 mph and the speed limit is 30 mph, you'll want to slow down. If you're buying curtains, you'll need to know some window measurements to help you decide how much material to order.

Measurement is used for control, improvement and communication. In many cases, there will be a threshold beyond which satisfactory turns into unsatisfactory, for example, expenditure up to your income level may be satisfactory, but above your income level, unsatisfactory, with remedial action needed. In other cases, present performance may be used as a starting point for future improvement.

Setting norms or target values is a skill based on experience and also, in many cases, comparison with others or with your own past performance.

Below are two examples of target setting:

1. IT service levels in contracts and SLAs are set to make sure the needs of the business are met, but may involve trade-offs as to how much the client organisation is prepared to pay to secure incremental improvements. When SLA targets are comfortably being exceeded, the client might ask for them to be tightened up, especially with an in-house provider.
2. Unit costs are often compared with industry norms, with these, in effect, becoming a target to be met or exceeded.

The actual measured values can be used, preferably in colour and graphic form, to show

how well we're doing, whether we're within target/tolerance and our direction of travel. There is an example later in the book (*see Figure 4*).

A word about terminology

In this book, when we use the term 'measure' as a noun, it is to refer both to things that are measured and to the measured value. By analogy with a tabletop, you can measure height, length and width, so height, length and width are useful measures for any tabletop. Their values for a particular tabletop might be: 75 cm, 140 cm and 70 cm respectively; so for that tabletop, the measures are height 75 cm, length 140 cm and width 70 cm.

'Measure' can also be used as a verb to mean performing the act of measuring and we will occasionally use it in that sense.

We will avoid the use of the word 'measure' to denote an action (or the performing of an action) that is not specifically related to measurement. So for example, we will use 'remedial actions' rather than 'remedial measures'.

A 'metric' is often likened to a measurement scale, so in this case the tabletop metrics are height, length and width measured in centimetres and the value of the metrics for this particular table are 75, 140 and 70. The term is often used synonymously with the use of 'measure' as a noun as described above; where we refer to metrics in this book, that is what we mean.

Do measures always have to be 'numeric' (quantitative)? In this book, the answer is no. We will use the term 'measure' to include assessments that are not necessarily numeric: for example, customer satisfaction may be rated on a five-point scale such as: very satisfied, satisfied, neither satisfied nor dissatisfied, dissatisfied and very dissatisfied, although it can help if they can be presented numerically. So in the example, a measurement system using 5, 4, 3, 2 and 1 may be more useful, especially for graphically presenting and manipulating management information on customer satisfaction.

Inputs, outputs and outcomes

IT measurement applies to inputs, outputs and, to a greater or lesser extent, outcomes.

Any business activity takes up resources, undertakes processes and generates outputs, which may in turn make possible or make easier the achievement of business outcomes. A supermarket:

- employs people and buys products and services (its inputs);
- provides products and customer-oriented services in its stores and online (its outputs);

and thereby:

- makes such-and-such profit and achieves such-and-such market share (its outcomes).

The organisation's senior management needs to keep its eye on the inputs, outputs and outcomes:

- inputs need to be kept to the minimum necessary to achieve business objectives, taking a longer-term strategic view wherever appropriate;

- outputs need to be good and innovative enough to keep customers happy and to drive achievement of desired outcomes, again taking an appropriately strategic perspective.

A client business will want to ensure that the time, effort and, especially, money it spends on IT are no higher than industry norms, unless there is a staggeringly good reason why, and that the IT that it receives meets business and user needs and contributes to business success.

An IT provider will want to ensure its resourcing is as efficient as possible, its client charges are competitive and its offerings are well received by clients. The provider will want its services to enable the provider's own success; at the same time, it will want itself to be perceived as contributing effectively to its clients' business success.

The provider's task of measuring its IT is more onerous than the clients': the provider has to have an eye on all its clients' needs, which means measurement, as well as on day-to-day, medium-term and strategic IT performance. We will come back to these matters later.

Relation to key performance indicators

Key performance indicators (KPIs) are measures used in the governance of organisations and units to provide managers and external stakeholders with essential (key) information on the performance of the organisation.

KPIs are chosen to reflect what is important to the organisation, for example, for reasons of assessment, control, improvement or communications. Each KPI has a target, the achievement of which shows whether performance against that indicator can be deemed successful. For example, the performance of an IT department in successfully resolving incidents could be judged by whether it does so on time for at least 95 per cent of the incidents, so the KPI in this case is 95 per cent on-time closure. What constitutes 'on time' would be set to reflect client needs, with incidents of differing seriousness having different time-to-resolve targets against which on-time performance would be judged.

When you measure your IT, you need to measure your KPIs for IT. There will probably be other things you want to measure, too, as you will read later in this book.

KPIs are not the same as organisational goals or objectives, but their values may indicate how to be more successful at meeting these goals either now or in the future. A goal for an insurance company might be a 10 per cent increase in business, to which achievement of its IT-related KPIs (such as 99.8 per cent customer availability) might contribute.

Relation to health checks

If you go to the doctor for a health check, the doctor will use measurements, e.g. temperature, heart rate and blood pressure. The doctor may also check for the existence of certain symptoms and may check your records to see if your body is missing some of the features that you'd expect to have.

Health checks such as benchmarks, IT capability maturity assessments and certifications to quality management standards are used to assess organisations' achievement against defined performance levels and, in the latter two cases, the maturity and repeatability of their processes.

In other words, health checks are measurements of particular aspects of performance, against definitions of 'what good looks like'. Are you super-fit and living healthily?

Relation to auditing

Auditing is used to check for compliance with standards and procedures. It is also used to help detect inadequate governance, fraud and corruption.

Auditing involves inspection of records and interviewing of people. It can involve scrutiny of things that would get measured anyway such as expenditure. It can also involve scrutiny of things that are measured specifically for auditing purposes, such as the percentage of software on the system that is correctly licensed.

Unexpected measurements can be an indication of non-compliance or worse. For example, if an inspection of the hardware and software on the system does not match the inventory, it may indicate that there have been unauthorised purchases or some other irregularity.

The trending of audit measurements, such as the percentage of correctly licensed software over time, can be a useful means of showing whether probity and compliance are improving over time. Action can be taken to address areas where improvement is needed.

Compliance and conformance

As mentioned above, you can use measurement to check the extent of compliance with standards and procedures. You can also check compliance with contracts and SLAs.

Don't be tempted to measure compliance with frameworks like ITIL®, though. Frameworks aren't generally defined tightly enough to allow you to say you're complying with them and have measurements to demonstrate compliance. You can set up your procedures in conformity with a framework like ITIL, but it's the procedures with which you comply, not the framework, and so it's compliance with the procedures that you can measure; it's against the procedures that you can audit.

Warning! Measure what is important

Whether you work for the IT provider or the client business, you need to measure (or assess) what is important to your organisation. What is important isn't always easy to measure; conversely, what is easy to measure isn't always important. Always bear in mind that measurement is a means to an end – effective or better IT, in this case – and never an end in itself. How comprehensively we can measure doesn't automatically lead to business success; indeed too much measurement would be a waste of effort.

What you measure really needs the blessing of appropriately senior, responsible management in your organisation. These are the people who will be in a position to act on what the measurements are telling them. They should have enough knowledge and wisdom to steer against measuring the wrong things, or measuring them in isolation, and so optimising the wrong things. For example, an isolated measure on the time to close incidents without dealing with the time it takes to fix the underlying cause may drive perverse behaviour. Thus, an IT department could close an incident stemming from a recurring fault by providing an awkward circumvention and so make the incident closure statistics look good, but annoy its customers by not sorting out the underlying cause. The business and the IT provider should want IT optimised for their respective and common needs; they don't, as a rule, want isolated aspects of IT provision optimised in their own right.

You will need to involve relevant stakeholders in deciding what to suggest to senior management is measured – unless senior management tells you, in which case it should have consulted the stakeholders! It is recognised good practice to use workshops to decide on an organisation's measurements. These workshops should be led by managers with enough authority to make decisions that stick and by people competent in steering sensible decisions on measurement.

Beware blips

If you measured how you feel every hour of every day, you might see a lot of ups and downs. You'd be unwise to seek psychiatric help just because you felt miserable for half an hour because you needed a cup of coffee. But if you felt miserable every day for six months, you might want to get some help. So how often you measure depends on what you're measuring. And it needs judgement to decide how quickly you need to react to what you are seeing. If you're responsible for buying umbrellas for a department store, you wouldn't do it on the strength of an isolated light shower, but rather you'd base your decision on historical statistics and, perhaps, longer-range weather forecasts; on the other hand, if you had umbrellas in the storeroom and a shower started, you'd put them out for sale.

Keep it proportionate

It's a statement of the obvious that you should not spend more on measuring than you'll realise in benefits as a result of the measurement. In fact, with IT skills at a premium, you probably want to spend a whole lot less on measurement than you'd expect to gain from it. Don't make an industry out of it! You can always come back and look at things in more detail if the need arises, particularly if you've planned your approach to measurement with flexibility in mind.

FOR MY £35,000 SALARY, I'VE SAVED US £20,000 THIS YEAR.

Figure 1: Keep it proportionate!

Put measurement in safe hands

Measurement is a powerful means of assessing and presenting the truth about things that are measurable. Its reliability depends on the quality of the tools used and of the individuals using them.

Be wary not just of mistakes and competence shortfalls, but also of measurements that are deliberately falsified or embellished. For example:

- a provider could try to suggest it's complying better with the contract than it really is;
- a health check could be skewed to show the unit concerned is in a better state than it really is.

So don't entrust measurement to individuals whose work is never checked. If in doubt about a set of measurements, ask for proof.

CHAPTER 2: THE BUSINESS PERSPECTIVE ON YOUR IT

Oh would some power the giftie gie us, to see ourselves as others see us. *To A Louse* (Robert Burns, 1786).

Before diving into the business's interest in IT measurement, let's consider some business perspectives on IT. The business's perspectives aren't always comfortable for the IT provider. All the business wants is for the required IT to be there whenever needed, for the price to represent value for money and for changes and problems to be dealt with efficiently: surely not too much to ask? Yet the providers can seem not very understanding, defensively hiding behind the contract: 'our stats show the service is fine' when the users would regard it as anything but fine.

Actually, in many businesses that particular 'want' is only a starting point; IT is also expected to enable business change by allowing things to be done more efficiently, or by allowing completely new things to be done. Let's walk before we run, though, and hide that complexity in the words 'required IT'.

As we shall see later, measurement provides a common language that helps client and provider to understand each other's point of view, to be clear about what's actually going well, to see what their differences are and to do something about it.

For now, let us listen to some 'customers'. Although the comments in this book are in no case a single individual's, everything quoted has been said within your author's hearing, by real people in equivalent roles. In case you think one of them is you, he has rubbed shoulders with many people in many different organisations!

A business manager comments:

I'm absolutely fed up with the company that runs our IT.

When you phone up the help desk, they're polite enough but you get nothing but platitudes. They're getting slightly better now at twigging that when they get 20 calls about the same thing that it actually is the same thing. But they still haven't woken up to the possibility when they get 20 calls that it might be serious – please fix now! I'm working my socks off to immovable deadlines (like, 20 minutes from now) and they're not sure if the disaster unfolding before them needs to be given priority, but they'll ask our customer services rep when the rep gets into the office in the next hour or so. Well thank you, I'll just get on with having a nervous breakdown while we wait.

Then there was that six-hour 'non-availability' in November. Our money was pouring out and no income was coming in. Goodwill was haemorrhaging, our reputation in tatters. 'Sorry', the company said. 'We took a while to realise how serious it was and our plan to honour our obligation to have you up and running in 30 minutes didn't work as we'd intended'. That's if you believe they had a plan. Hopefully somebody has made sure they have one now and hopefully it works. But, on past performance, I have no confidence. I haven't been overly impressed with our own IT department's ability to manage this company either. The company just seems to be getting money for old rope.

They sent out their customer director a couple of weeks ago to spend a day with us. She was really understanding and she's pledged to get things done in the company. The question is: will she?

I don't suppose I'll ever get a chance to decide who provides our IT. But if I do ever get any influence over it, I'll do my utmost to bring in somebody else.

Seem familiar?

Not everybody rants like that, but IT is an emotive subject.

When your author and his team were thinking about developing ITIL 25 years ago, we were concerned about 'growing dependence on IT'. We had no idea, though, just how dependent organisations and their staff, customers and stakeholders would be on IT. Lose the connection to the Internet and many people can scarcely do business; lose IT completely and the staff may as well go home. Reputations, services, profitability and careers all hinge on being able to rely on IT.

So, first and foremost, *business managers* want:

- their IT to be on-stream and working 'as advertised';
- to know, when things go wrong, that they'll be fixed quickly. Minutes of deprivation may be a fact of life; hours of deprivation are unacceptable;
- chronic problems to be addressed. Where the service 'as advertised' isn't dealing effectively with chronic problems, they want something to be done.

A finance director comments:

We weren't party to the setting up of this IT contract; we're just a minor user of our holding company's contract with company A. Frankly, I'd never have agreed to it.

The service itself isn't too bad. The company more or less meets the terms of the contract, although I know quite a few of our users grumble about the service. I say 'more or less' because there was one spectacular six-hour break a few weeks ago that excited our Board and left quite a lot of people very miffed. Most people are just resigned to this kind of thing being a fact of life. They don't forget, but they quickly put it behind them.

We've also had complaints about their help desk being 'nice but dim': lovely people, but ineffective at getting problems dealt with.

What really gets my goat though is that I know we're being ripped off. We're paying for fat-cat executive salaries, for sales and marketing that are of no interest to us and for company profits being channelled back to corporate headquarters.

When you look at the cost of a desktop (well it's a laptop these days, actually) it's astronomical. Thank goodness we aren't in the public sector because I'd hate to be asked a Freedom of Information [*http://www.legislation.gov.uk/ukpga/2000/36/ contents*] question about this; we'd look really stupid. As it is, I just can't believe we're paying so much.

Are you being ripped off?

Uncomfortable question, isn't it? If only there were a gauge you could use to show you if you're getting value for money. It's not that simple, of course, any more than it's simple to know if your car's fuel consumption is economical. In fact, the car example is simpler because experts can test different cars in the same conditions, so enabling like to be compared with like. Unfortunately, you can't take your IT to a test site and compare its value for money with other people's IT.

The costs of your IT will depend on what's expected to be covered. Typically, the operation and support of infrastructure and supported applications are covered. If you break the costs down that way, it makes it easier to compare like-for-like with other organisations. The acquisition and tailoring of new applications should be costed separately and so may be charged separately. Changes above a minimum level are also likely to be costed and charged separately. And therein lies a tale in its own right.

At one time, it was legendary that IT outsourcing companies would bid low and make up for the shortfall through charges for the inevitable changes that clients would always need. Don't be fooled that this practice has disappeared! Guard against it through your skill and your understanding of the market.

Finance directors are most interested in:

- IT units costs in the steady state;
- cost of changes;
- whether the above represent value for money.

Programmes and projects

IT enables us to change the way we work – faster, cheaper, more efficiently and in a more customer-friendly way – and to do new things. So, inevitably, we need to buy or develop new applications. The acquisition projects delivering these applications are prone to lateness, cost overruns and scope change, which aren't always the fault of the provider. They often sit within a programme designed to bring about IT-related business change. In other words, it isn't just a matter of delivering software, there will also be a need for business process changes, user readiness, go-live planning, and so on. Programmes and projects present client businesses with a whole new set of management challenges that measurement supports.

A business manager comments:

What a shambles. The project manager going on and on and on about how clever he was and how he'd never delivered a late project. 'Pity about the suppliers', he said, 'incompetent and showing precious little commitment'. He had the project teams working night and day to get the software in on time. 'The project was 110 per cent successful and reflects very well on us as an organisation. Let's invite the press in to let them see how good we are'. But wait a minute. The business wasn't happy: it was the wrong answer delivered early and it would never work, not even if we got everybody to stand on their heads. The project manager just couldn't see it. To him all that mattered was delivery on time and to quality.

The business (the Board) is interested in:

- successful IT-enabled change programmes, with
- projects delivering to time, to budget and to quality (or rather to its 'need', without going over budget or delivering too late).

Strategic alignment

If you run your own IT, it's pretty straightforward for the Board to set a direction for IT that aligns with where the business is heading and that will give the business a helping hand. If somebody else runs your IT, the two sides need to understand each other's direction well enough to decide whether to keep the relationship going, fine-tuning it if needed, or to consider a parting of the ways. The business requirement for IT will change over time, as the business and supporting infrastructure and technologies evolve. The existing provider can only stay credible if it keeps pace with changing needs and opportunities – reacting to what the business wants to do and how it wants to use IT, and proposing solutions to business needs that are both stated and unstated.

The business is likely to be interested, as a minimum, in:

- the provider's strategic IT capability being maintained;
- the effectiveness of two-way communications to ensure business and IT alignment.

Pulling it all together

Figure 2 shows in simple form how measurement can be used in several ways to assess and improve your IT, starting at the top right:

- to direct its improvement;
- to intervene when things need to be corrected or changed;
- to demonstrate performance and/or justify cases for more resources, etc.;
- to show progress against strategy implementation and validate direction of travel.

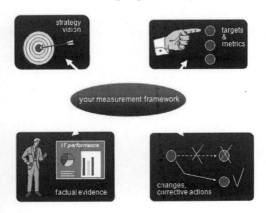

Figure 2: Why measure?

When your organisation has mastered IT measurement, you'll be able to devise your own measurement framework, linked to your own business and IT needs.

CHAPTER 3: THE IT PROVIDER'S PERSPECTIVE ON YOUR IT

The best way to find yourself is to lose yourself in the service of others. Mahatma Ghandi

Service roles can be rather thankless. The provider's job of satisfying customers by meeting contractual or SLA obligations and providing value for money is not easy, being dependent on infrastructure, vendors, business processes and customer relationships. The service is usually highly visible to customers and their expectations tend to be high. IT services are business-critical, prone to requests for change and improvement, and prone to faults. From the IT provider's perspective, customers often want more and better, and they can't tell you precisely what they do want, but they're pretty quick to say what they don't want. So IT service provision can be particularly challenging.

The fictitious commentator below represents real opinions that IT provider staff have expressed, either to your author or in his earshot, about third-party organisations that must remain anonymous.

An IT provider comments:

Well, I've just about had enough of this client. The users only ever tell us what's wrong. We're working our socks off with flaky technology to provide them with actually quite a good service that usually far exceeds their mediocre contract terms. When the occasional problem does arise, we usually close it well within deadline, though we did admittedly have an exceptional outage last November, which took us the wrong side of compliance. We've now resolved the underlying problem, so it won't happen again. The customers are far too quick to tell us what they don't want, or don't like, and never very clear on what they do want or need. Half the time when things go wrong it's their fault anyway.

They expect us to deliver projects on time, yet they can't agree the spec, their senior managers don't turn up to meetings, decisions are made without them and then they undo the decisions. It's so annoying. How can we work like that?

We're expected to reduce costs from year to year, but quite honestly it's a pure fluke we've been able to do it. Luckily we've taken on new customers that we've been able to service without raising our headcount. That's because we managed to iron out a lot of faults, so we didn't get the increase in support enquiries you might have expected with a bunch of new users, which would have strained our capacity.

Mind you, we do have one or two model clients who make up for the hassle we get with the others.

Wanted: a quiet life?

IT providers generally want:

- customer satisfaction;
- to meet their obligations under their contracts or SLAs;
- to be perceived as offering value for money, which can be a prerequisite for repeat business;
- to deliver projects within budget and to customer satisfaction;
- to be seen as offering a responsive service, with efficient handling of problems;
- to be on top of risks;
- to keep a step ahead by being able to offer more and better, without demanding more payment for it;
- to have an inside track with their customers, so that new business opportunities come their way;
- in all the respects above, to be better than IT providers that are, or could become, competitors.

Paddling below the water line

Those responsible for IT provision will have things to measure and deal with that will contribute to meeting these customer-driven wants. Just like the garage looking after your car, the IT provider needs to look after what's going on under the bonnet – the provider's infrastructure and processes.

For example, providers will want to know the following:

- if the IT equipment or software is unreliable, meaning it needs to be replaced or repaired;

3: The IT provider's perspective on your IT

- if the users don't know how to use it, meaning they need to be asked to learn;
- if the IT isn't secure, meaning it needs to be made secure;
- if the processes for managing the IT configuration don't keep it under control, meaning they need to be changed so that they do.

CHAPTER 4: MEASUREMENT COMMON GROUND FOR CLIENT AND PROVIDER?

Things would run a lot more smoothly if we didn't have the passengers to contend with.
Anonymous rail manager

Providing an IT service is a bit like running a train service. People soon know when things go wrong and they tend not to be very patient about it. They just expect things to work like a Swiss watch. And everybody thinks it's simple. Yet, behind the scenes, it needs reliable hardware and software and constant management attention, with well-defined processes, both to minimise problems and to deal with them efficiently when they do arise.

Measurement can be the glue holding things together. So long as there is a willingness on both sides, it can provide a common vocabulary that helps customer and provider to understand what the customer is getting. However, if the trade-offs and constraints involved in deciding acceptable service levels have not been made plain to enable user buy-in, measurement will probably just highlight unresolved differences that need to be reconciled before it can be used as a beneficial tool.

What are the numbers telling you?

A train passenger comments:

'All I want is for them to run on time. As it is you have to get up an hour earlier than you should, just to make sure you get to your meetings on time. And when you get delays, they never tell you till you're a captive audience and you can't go another way. You're lucky if they tell you what's gone wrong and they always say it'll be fixed faster than it really is. I'm surprised they don't lose the franchise because they're awful.'

A train company manager responds:

'We're actually achieving good punctuality and reliability figures, well above the contractual requirement. We're committed to delivering the best possible service because that way we improve our revenues, we grow our business and we're more likely, with a good reputation, to win the franchise again. We've put a lot of effort into fleet reliability, which is now very good, and we're working more closely than ever with the rail infrastructure company to address the remaining track and signalling issues. Our operational practices are proven to be effective. Our incident and problem management is well developed, so when things do go wrong we deal with both the immediate impact and the underlying cause. The figures bear it out.'

An independent observer comments:

'What we aren't being told is that the communication between provider and customers isn't as good as it should be. The company does an annual customer satisfaction survey and the results show this every single time. The hard measures show things are fine (though there's always room for improvement) but the soft customer measures have a different story to tell. Both sides actually have access to a common set of figures that show that service is perfectly respectable, but customer care and communications are in need of improvement. All they need to do is understand the numbers and act on what the numbers are telling them.'

Align your goals

In this book, a key theme is the alignment of client and provider measures, around what both sides expect of IT provision.

It's surprising how often you hear of misalignment, even with an internal provider, for example:

- IT and business goals not aligned;
- the business is dissatisfied with IT facilities;
- IT quality and change-handling are putting the business at risk.

4: Measurement common ground for client and provider?

While measurement will help to identify and diagnose delivery problems, it can't resolve a failure to line up IT and business goals in the first place. Indeed, if you don't line these up, there is an increased risk of using measurement to prop up the wrong decisions!

Inputs, outputs and outcomes

Let us further consider measurement of inputs, outputs and outcomes, which we introduced earlier. IT, like any business activity, has inputs and outputs, which are pivotal to provider/client relationships. IT inputs and outputs contribute to client outcomes; just as importantly, but of less interest in a chapter on common ground, IT inputs and outputs also contribute to provider outcomes like profitability and repeat business.

What constitutes an input and what constitutes an output depends on your perspective. Inputs are the resources used to do the work. For an IT service providing support to one or more businesses, the inputs will include the IT provider staff, the hardware and software, and the funding to pay for them.

The outputs will be the service, which will be expected to comply with the contract or SLA. The handling of change requests, problems and complaints will be included as service outputs, probably measured as volumes handled and statistics on efficiency of handling (e.g. on-time closure). The outputs are in effect the IT provided to the business.

4: Measurement common ground for client and provider?

Inputs tend to be common across most IT service provision, with quantitative variations (e.g. in annual costs) reflecting things like scale of operation, efficiency and customer requirements. Many IT service outputs are qualitatively common across customer organisations, but there are variations in the subset of generic services provided (e.g. application development).

Businesses are also interested in outcomes – the effects of the IT on the business it is supporting and, typically, on the business's customers, for example, the number of new accounts opened or of mortgages let. The outcomes reflect what the service is being provided for, so are much more customer-specific than inputs and outputs. But it is important for the IT provider to understand what the customer outcomes are expected to be, even if they are not contractual; this is because the business is quite likely to judge the IT provider on whether the IT supports the business's fundamental drivers.

Summing up, the business and the provider will be interested in common measures of outputs (compliance with SLA/contract), some input measures, especially costs, and in fulfilment of outcomes. Achievement of client outcomes will probably be measurable, but the IT provider's part in contributing to client outcomes may not be very amenable to measurement.

The provider is highly likely to need additional measures to show how effectively it is operating, including measures concerned with its own processes.

4: Measurement common ground for client and provider?

Overlapping perspectives

Beauty is in the eye of the beholder. Origin obscure.

Funder's perspective

The IT client organisation, whose business will probably depend on IT, will want to define what it is to get for its money and check that it gets it, typically in terms of:

- services
- availability and reliability
- capacity
- customer service
- responsiveness to change and problems.

Some form of customer satisfaction check may be included in the client organisation's assessment of whether it is getting what it is paying for.

User's perspective

The users want a service that performs as advertised. Actually they probably want better than that, but their absolute expectation – or hope – will be 'reliably available and usable'. Then there's the question of whether it supports what they need to do. How does the provider treat users when things go wrong? How does it handle the situation generally when things go wrong? Does it fix faults, or do the users have to complain about the same things over and over again? How does the provider handle change? Does the bill mean the users are getting value for money?

4: Measurement common ground for client and provider?

Provider's perspective

The provider's main purpose is to serve. It will probably have financial constraints, such as overall or unit cost ceilings, and it may have revenue targets related to the service being provided. It will generally want to provide a service that meets or exceeds the commitments in the contract or SLA and, at the same time, satisfy or delight customers and stakeholders.

Thus, the provider will want to run the services as advertised or slightly better than that. It'll want people to be satisfied with customer care, especially when there are changes and problems. But it lives in the real world. The funding available may not stretch to providing everybody with what they ideally would like. Things do go wrong and people get frustrated. How these realities are addressed, and how good customer communications are, will then be of pivotal importance.

The stakeholders and customers have no real interest in the details underpinning an effective performance. The provider, on the other hand, must track those aspects that underpin performance and affect both the quality of service provided and the cost of provision. Things like quality and availability of staff and reliability of infrastructure (mean time between failure and time to fix) will contribute to a reliable performance. The time taken to restore normality after service faults will directly affect customers, but the time taken to deal with underlying problems, which is essential information for the provider, may only be of passing interest to the customer.

The IT provider will need to track performance against the measures of interest to customers and other stakeholders, and also be on top of things like change, problem and incident management performance, infrastructure availability and reliability, people performance and productivity.

Providers may need to delve deeper into their processes to check if they are effective, efficient and repeatable. Process repeatability is important for quality and efficiency; the alternative is for staff to keep reinventing the wheel, which costs money and is unreliable. Compliance with process standards and process effectiveness and efficiency will be of particular concern, if they are suspected of being below par.

What are the measures in common?

The business using IT, its funders and users all share an interest with the provider in measures of service quality and cost. We'll look at these in more detail later, but they will typically include (but not necessarily be limited to) adherence to contractual (or SLA) obligations, which themselves could include some or all of the following:

- percentage availability of the service;
- percentage availability of key applications;
- incidence and duration of outages and other significant incidents, categorised by incident severity (incident duration statistics are

sometimes expressed as mean time to fix).
Note that the related statistic on the mean time
to fix underlying problems, which has an
impact on incident frequency because an
unresolved problem can cause an incident to
recur, is often of no interest to the client
organisation, although it ought to be of interest
if the service is unstable;

- delivery performance of projects and changes:
  on time, to specification (or customer
  satisfaction) and to budget? Depending on the
  nature and make-up of the project, this
  indicator can be a reflection of client-side
  behaviour as well as provider performance.
  For example, if the client organisation keeps
  changing its requirements or is unavailable to
  make key decisions when they are scheduled,
  then it should not be surprised if the project
  goes over time or over budget;

- value for money, assessed through statistics
  like cost per user and project/change
  efficiency;

- customer satisfaction, assessed through a
  standardised, repeatable measure
  (questionnaire).

As we saw earlier, there will quite likely be a
desire for the client's and provider's IT-related
interests to be strategically aligned. That is an
aspect of the relationship, however, that isn't
readily assessed by measurement.

The people on the provider side responsible for
driving and improving performance, and for
achieving the best possible value for money, will

need more measures than those above to guide their work.

In the rest of this book, we'll look in more detail at measurements for client and provider, illustrated with some examples.

The focus of measurement depends on the context

Whereas both client and provider will have a common interest in the generic measures just outlined, the *focus* of attention for both will depend on the context.

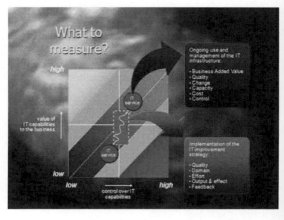

Figure 3: Measurement focus

Figure 3 neatly illustrates the importance of context. If the business's control of the IT on which it depends is low, then it needs to get a grip.

4: Measurement common ground for client and provider?

Maybe the provider needs to get a grip too – or maybe the client needs to get a grip on the provider. Regardless, as shown in *Figure 3*, attention needs to be paid to implementing IT improvement, which means measuring and acting on:

- IT quality
- IT domains (areas of focus)
- effort/resources deployed
- outputs and outcomes
- customer and staff feedback.

If the client needs to secure better business value from its IT, then both client and provider need to be able to assess and act on the following aspects of the client's IT:

- business added value (is it doing as much for our business as it could?)
- quality
- effective handling of business- and IT-engendered change
- capacity management
- cost management
- overall control.

These focuses aren't either/or. You need to control your IT *and* improve its business value. You can't easily do the latter if you haven't brought your IT under reasonable control. But you should pay particular attention to your most significant challenge.

CHAPTER 5: WHAT THE BUSINESS NEEDS TO MEASURE

He who pays the piper calls the tune. Origin obscure.

Let's start our more detailed look at measurement on the client side. Any business will be interested in whether:

- it is getting the service as contracted (or as detailed in the SLA);
- value for money is being achieved;
- the business and its users are happy and getting what they need;
- problems are properly dealt with;
- changes, small and big, including 'projects', are handled effectively;
- IT plans allow the business to keep 'a step ahead'.

This is not a definitive list for all businesses. Many will be interested in other things besides.

To be in control of these requirements, the business needs to have regular measurements or assessments of how things stand and how they're trending (e.g. getting better, getting worse, erratic and the like).

For illustration, *Figure 4* shows an example report on compliance with an SLA.

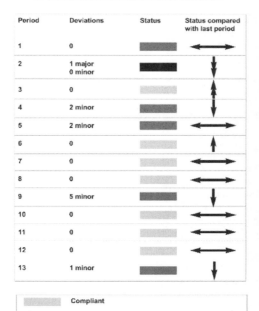

Figure 4: Example SLA compliance report

A board member comments:

Don't talk to me about IT measurement. We've been using this IT company, let's call them ICTPROVID, for years.

We keep hearing about radically different IT infrastructure based on Cloud Computing, apps, open standards, smaller projects and a lot more SMEs in the supply chain. I can't see much sign of it. For us, it's very much a case of 'same old, same old'.

What I'd like to know is how the prices we're paying compare with what other organisations using ICTPROVID pay: are we all in the same boat or are some of them getting better commercial arrangements? I'd like to compare us with organisations that aren't using ICTPROVID, too, to see if they fare better. I know they say you can't just compare one client organisation with another by looking at cost per user (what they used to call cost per desktop before we all migrated to laptops), but the comparisons I've seen suggest we're getting a shabby deal. Admittedly, things have got a bit better since we renegotiated with the company, but there's still a way to go.

It'd be interesting to look at customer satisfaction because we hear a lot of grumbles about there being too many niggling faults and that they aren't being resolved quickly enough. You always get grumbles about IT, but we could do with some stats to confirm whether there's actually any substance to the complaints about ICTPROVID. I know some of our users feel the contract doesn't give them what they need, so some of the niggles may be in grey areas where the company's performance complies with the contract, which means we're between a rock and a hard place, as we're unhappy to live with it, but don't want to pay through the nose to get it changed.

We've been thankfully free of the IT project disasters that have afflicted some public sector organisations, but, at the same time, you can't rely on them to deliver what they say they're going to deliver at the time they promise. Again, I don't know how we compare with others and it would be useful to have some meaningful stats to let us know.

Contract management seems to be a black art, with the commercial and IT folk united in reassuring the Board that ICTPROVID fully complies with the terms of the contract. That makes me question the effectiveness of the contract. I'd like to see the facts and figures.

Let us turn to that well-known phrase or saying: continuous improvement. Is ICTPROVID performing better for us this year than last? Is it performing better for others this year than last? Are we getting enough year-on-year improvement? Are others? Can we find out?

A business manager in the same organisation comments:

I'm reasonably happy with the service we get from ICTPROVID, which makes me a bit of a rarity around here. The IT service is mostly quite reliable, I've got a nice laptop that's easy to take on the train although the battery life isn't much cop, and we now have e-mail access when we're travelling, which is a major step forward. The facilities I use, like e-mail, word processing, spreadsheets and presentation slides, all work smoothly. The finance and HR systems are a bit of a pain, with yet more passwords to remember, but that isn't ICTPROVID's fault.

Where I do have a complaint with ICTPROVID is when things go wrong. We often work to very tight deadlines and we've had a couple of instances in the last six months when the service has died on us at the worst possible time. One of the failures lasted six hours and the other one was the best part of 20 hours. That time, ICTPROVID ended up having to bring people in from elsewhere in the country. Now they did send out their account director, a really nice person, to explain what had gone wrong and what they were doing to make sure it wouldn't happen again. To the account director's credit, it hasn't. But when you've been let down that badly, it leaves a sour taste in the mouth.

Another thing I find disturbing about them is their service desk. The people are friendly enough; that's not the problem. It's just that they're inefficient. For instance, we came in one morning to find we couldn't access e-mails or the Internet, so the service was next to useless. I phoned the service desk and they said they would log the call. When I pressed whether they'd heard about the problem, they admitted they had, which was just as well as my friends sitting beside me said they'd already phoned in about the problem. But here's the rub: the service desk were waiting for the number of calls logged about the problem to reach, say, 20 (I can't remember the exact figure) before escalating it to category one. I can just about see their perspective; one user experiencing this problem could be down to that user. But three or four users with the same symptoms: wake up and smell the coffee!

Another organisation's board member comments:

We run our own IT department because we don't trust anybody else to do it and, frankly, it's too important to the business to do anything else. With an in-house IT department, we can control the direction of IT in the company: we decide what it does and how much we're prepared to spend. We can say 'jump' and expect to be asked 'how high'? We say how much we're prepared to spend and we decide whether we're getting what we pay for.

I'm not saying we're by any means perfect. The IT folk have a bad habit of changing things without telling you, which would be fine if their changes didn't affect us, but you end up wasting time chasing answers to niggling faults or to changes to the way you have to use the system. To their credit, they're pretty good at fixing problems once identified, so we don't get a lot of repeat faults.

The service desk is friendly and efficient, so if you do have a complaint or query it's dealt with politely and effectively.

Strategic-level changes and projects are agreed at Board level. Sometimes they're proposed by the IT department and sometimes they come out of strategic reviews. It means the business and the IT department are singing from the same song sheet, so the conditions are set for projects to succeed. That's not to say projects always come in to spec or time or budget. But on the whole we're satisfied with the way the business handles IT projects.

Measures for the business: checklist

Note that when IT is externally provided, what the client can require to be measured and what it can demand to be done about the findings will depend on what's in the contract. Regardless, the business should ask for a regular report on contract or SLA compliance, which should draw on the measurements discussed below.

Service availability

What

- The percentage of scheduled time that service is available for use.
- This may include figures categorised by location, where the service provision covers more than one site.
- This may include availability of each important application, measured as a percentage of scheduled time for which the application is available.
- This may include a separate measure of down time (or down time per location, or per key application) over a certain threshold. For example, the business may only require a

report on service outages of over one hour, measured along these lines:

o   frequency and length of business-critical outages of one hour or more.

o   At the same time, if location A would struggle after 30 minutes of down time, the business could ask for a report on location A service outages of 30 minutes or more.

o   If the loss of application X was business-critical after four hours, a report on the frequency and length of application X outages of four hours or more should be requested.

When

• Timing and frequency will depend on how big an issue availability is or has become. During a provider's first few months, statistics may be needed as often as once a week and covering a period as short as a week, whereas once the service is stable, monthly or quarterly figures may suffice. Equally, the frequency of gathering statistics may need to be ratcheted up and the service interval to be assessed shortened, if the service becomes unstable or at times of significant IT change.

• *Figures 5–8* show various ways of measuring and presenting service availability over a full year for a service scheduled to be online 168 hours a week, which was afflicted by two outages of 20 hours and six hours respectively. A longer measurement period of, say, three months, will give a smoother picture, with the blips ironed out, so making it easier to understand trend information (direction of travel). A three-month measurement period rolled forward every month (every four weeks) will provide overview and trend information faster than a set of back-to-back three-month measurements. But regardless, such a long period can mask availability problems that cause the business aggravation, and in that circumstance these measurements would need to be supplemented by more granular figures.

- *Table 1* shows the incidence and duration of service outages, for the same service. The client will probably want to see these only if availability is problematic.

Week Number	Number of Incidents	Duration per outage (hours)
1	0	
2	0	
3	3	2,3,3
4	1	1
5	0	
6	1	20
7	0	
8	0	
9	3	3,2,1
10	0	
11	0	
12	0	
13	0	
14	0	
15	1	1
16	0	
17	2	2,2
18	0	
19	0	
20	0	
21	3	4,1,1
22	0	
23	1	3
24	1	2
25	2	1 ½, 3 ½
26	0	
27	0	
28	0	
29	0	
30	1	4
31	0	
32	0	
33	3	1,1,1

34	0	
35	0	
36	1	6
37	0	
38	0	
39	0	
40	0	
41	0	
42	0	
43	1	1
44	0	
45	0	
46	1	2
47	0	
48	0	
49	0	
50	0	
51	1	2
52	0	

Table 1: Incidence and duration of service outages

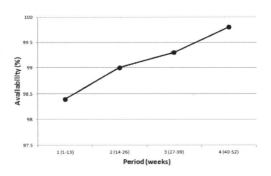

Figure 5: Availability chart: four 13-week periods

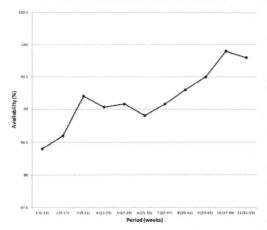

**Figure 6: Availability chart: 13-week
average rolled forward every four weeks**

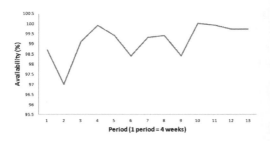

**Figure 7: Availability graph: 13 four-week
periods**

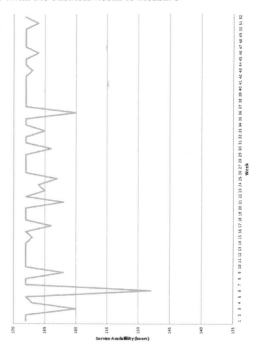

Figure 8: Weekly availability chart

Other service problems

What

- The measurements will comprise a summary of incidents affecting the service: organised by severity/priority and, if required, by problem category (e.g. security, capacity). The number of incidents and the time to close against target should be included for each severity level. It often has an accompanying explanatory report.

When

- The measurements will be best presented at the same time interval and covering the same duration as availability (typically monthly but can be quarterly for a stable service and can be more frequent for an unstable service or part of the service).
- *Table 2* and the graph in *Figure 9* show service incidents for the example service, in categories: security, capacity, configuration and release management. For simplicity, only one severity level is shown. The text accompanying the graph in *Figure 9* is a typical client report explaining the incidents.

Week	Security management	Capacity management	Configuration management	Release management
1	2	0	0	0
2	0	0	0	0
3	0	1	0	2
4	0	0	1	0
5	0	0	0	0
6	0	0	0	1
7	0	0	0	0
8	0	0	0	0

Table 2: Service incidents by category: example table

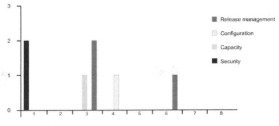

Explanation:
- 2 attempted hacking incidents – foiled
- 1 capacity problem causing slow running and service interruption – cause under investigation
- 3 problems with software instability following new release, 1 causing major outage
- 1 user report about an unregistered software asset

Figure 9: Example incident report: weeks 1–8

Customer satisfaction

What

- Some means of assessing customer satisfaction with the service, typically on a five-point scale, such as: very satisfied, satisfied, neither satisfied nor dissatisfied, dissatisfied and very dissatisfied.

The survey can be undertaken by the client on its own behalf. It really needs to be accompanied by open questions about what is and isn't good, to inform the client's management of its relationship with the provider. Inadequate communication between the provider and the users is a common cause of dissatisfaction. External and internal users can be covered by a combined survey or by separate surveys.

When

- This should typically be undertaken once a year, although twice a year or more often may be appropriate if the client's or users' satisfaction with the provider is low.

IT costs

What

A capable client will know from its finance department how much its IT is costing and may be more interested in statistics showing what (how much) it is getting for its money.

- For service operations, other things being equal, the cost per user provides a good indication of cost efficiency compared with others and compared with yourselves last time you measured it. Be careful to compare like with like, and include all the IT provider costs, unless there's a good reason to exclude them.
- One thing to single out by means of separate statistics is the cost of projects and other service changes, as the business needs to know how much it is paying for IT change without burying it as part of service operations. Where the business requirement is stable, the cost of change should be low. Particularly for projects, both provider and client costs should be of interest.

- Depending on the type of business, it may be illuminating to consider how well the breakdown of IT spend for normal operations and for IT-enabled business change aligns with the business's direction of travel. Thus, a smaller proportion of developmental spend this year compared with last in an organisation seeking IT-enabled advantage might suggest questions need to be asked.

When

- If IT budgets are under control, there is no need for the client to measure costs every five minutes. Depending on the provider's financial discipline and on service stability, a quarterly or even an annual report could be appropriate. If there is a lot of IT change, then more frequent measurement may be needed, perhaps as often as monthly, especially if the client is concerned about the cost of change.

Handling of change: projects

- Given the legendary costs of IT project failures, probably the two most interesting things to measure about projects are how much they cost (as above) and whether they're successful. What constitutes success isn't always as clear-cut as delivering to requirement, to time and to budget. These statistics are needed, but may need to be supplemented to reflect business judgements as to whether a slightly reduced scope or a slightly later delivery could be acceptable.

Post-project statistics on problems and changes affecting projects should be gathered for the benefit of future projects. Measurement of projects in-flight tends to follow a well-trodden path involving progress against milestones and budget and, often, statistics on problems and changes.

- In an organisation that undertakes a lot of projects, a portfolio assessment showing numbers of projects in gestation, planning, execution, testing, and so on, and time taken at each stage, will provide a useful view on what is going on and show any pinch points.

When

- Project measurement shouldn't just be left until the end. Progress against plan needs to be regularly tracked, to allow any corrective action to be taken. On completion, performance against requirement, time and budget should be reported; any deviation from requirement can be measured by assessing the number, or extent and seriousness, of deficiencies compared with requirement. A post-project assessment should be conducted some months after delivery, to check that required functions and benefits are being achieved.
- A regular projects report should be sought, typically once a quarter, but more or less often depending on the volume of projects and their success rate.

Handling of other changes

What

- Whereas any capable client will know what projects it has in the pipeline, in progress and delivered, and the planned and actual costs associated with each project, it may need to make a conscious effort to keep other service changes under control. The business should impose a strict cost ceiling on discretionary changes the provider can make without client approval. The client should request a regular report breaking down change costs per main system (application and infrastructure), to show where any stability problems are occurring.

When

- A quarterly report will often suffice, but the frequency can be stepped up or down depending on service stability. If the business is worried about particular systems, it can ask for more frequent reports and more detailed information, for example, on the sources of change requirements (e.g. error rectification, user request).

If you run your own IT

If you run your own IT, you'll need to take more interest in overseeing things that would otherwise be the provider's responsibility. Staffing is one such area, with things such as headcount, the wage bill and the staff's competence levels and development to be addressed. There are no absolutes to measure yourselves against, but you can join Special Interest Groups, enabling you to compare yourselves with others, and you can equally compare yourselves now with the way you were last year.

With an internal provider, the business will want to take a judicial interest in the aspects of IT management and measurement covered in our next chapter.

CHAPTER 6: WHAT IT PROVIDERS NEED TO MEASURE

An IT provider is interested in whether:

- the service is operating according to the contracts or SLAs it has with its clients;
- it is satisfying customers and is thus well regarded; it has effective strategic-level engagement with clients;
- it is perceived as offering value for money. More than that, it is actually operating efficiently and effectively;
- incidents and problems are being managed effectively with prompt resolutions and good customer communications;
- changes are handled well and introduced with either no or, at worst, few unwanted side effects;
- 'under the bonnet' processes are performing as they should; we come back to this topic in the next chapter.

An enlightened provider will also be interested in whether:

- it compares well with other providers;
- it is well positioned to meet future client needs.

All these performance indicators will need to be continually assessed and action taken to deal with any shortfalls.

There will be many aspects of a provider's own infrastructure and performance that contribute to an effective operation and so may need to be regularly assessed and tracked, for example:

- staffing: wage bill, headcount, capability and training;
- costs: in-depth breakdown showing operations and projects/changes separately;
- infrastructure and applications' stability: problem statistics, including incidences of recurrences;
- project performance: the number of projects at each stage of the life cycle and statistics on status at completion (whether to requirement, time and budget);
- incident/problem characteristics: severity and time to fix by system and by category, e.g. business continuity, security, capacity, testing and configuration;
- change characteristics: priority (significance) and time-to-close figures by system;
- handling of service transitions, e.g. success rates of introducing new software releases;
- whether it is keeping up to date with technologies.

A senior manager in ICTPROVID comments:

I see you've had comments about us from the Corporation. They're a pretty good bread-and-butter customer actually and we're giving them a pretty good service, with the service stats proving it. The contract is just past the midpoint, so we might start to feel the pressure in the next year or two, as they begin working towards a new contract. It's pretty likely the stakes will be higher next time round, with a group-wide contract the most likely choice. At the same time, they have a lot of commercially more savvy people nowadays, so they'll be expecting good prices through the life of the contract.

We bid low for the present contract, but we've made money on changes, as you'd expect, and through the familiar let-and-forget culture, so what was good value for money three years ago is now pretty mediocre, which, in the short term, is good for us, of course, but bad for them.

We get a bit of hassle from the Corporation about service problems, but they really haven't a leg to stand on. Our service is usually well within the contractual requirements, but their contract is so iffy that they didn't make provision for stuff that their users regard as essential. We do what we can to help, but they aren't prepared to dig into their pockets to amend the contract and we aren't in a position to act as if we're a charity.

We had a couple of really serious outages affecting one of their locations, which shouldn't have happened. One of them was caused by a piece of ropey software dating from years back that we knew might play up, but you know what they say: if it ain't broke, don't fix it! The other one, which was far worse and took the best part of a day to fix, was to do with a hardware single point of failure; in other words, an accident waiting to happen. We're having to pay a forfeit for the outage which is costing us more than preventing the problem would have done in the first place. That's apart from the reputational damage: lesson learned!

An IT delivery director comments:

The Corporation take the biscuit. We're providing a reliable service, with excellent service stats showing we're performing comfortably better than contract. Yet they're forever complaining about things they say they need that they didn't bother to get covered in the contract. Imagine how my staff feel about this: undermined, undervalued and unjustly criticised.

Mind you, we did have a couple of spectacular own goals, which did our reputation no favours whatsoever. The worse of the two was an incident caused by a hardware fault that was reported at 7.25 am on a Wednesday and wasn't fixed till 3 am the next morning. It would have been so easy to provide a hot standby, which I actually had asked for, but got turned down. I don't want to say we're skinflints, but we've ended up having to fork out more in compensation than it would have cost us to prevent the problem in the first place. The other incident lasted about six hours; it was caused by a problem with legacy software that would have been hard to prevent without replacing or re-engineering the application. So it probably was the right decision to leave it. However, we should have been more prepared to act quickly when things went wrong with it – a lesson I hope we've now learned.

Essential measures for providers: checklist

Some of the measures suggested here reflect those
suggested for the client side. To ensure the service
is under control, the provider will generally need
to gauge things more frequently than the client.

Staff

What

- The provider needs to keep an eye on its staff
  numbers and wage bill. If external resources
  are used, for example, temporary staff or
  consultants, their numbers and costs should be
  monitored.
- Staff skills and competencies should be
  regularly assessed against those required, with
  action taken to deal with shortfalls. The
  average amount of training undertaken per
  person can be a useful indicator that staff
  members are being developed. However,
  having a target of a certain number of training
  days per person per year isn't necessarily the
  best way of fostering staff development; it
  depends on what the staff need and that should
  be decided person by person.

When

- Headcount and staff costs should be tracked
  frequently, say monthly, unless there are good
  reasons to the contrary. Competencies, training
  and development should be reviewed in
  accordance with the staff appraisal cycle.

Compliance with SLA or contract

What

- The provider needs to ensure it complies with the provisions of the SLA or contract. Typically, the requirements will cover the things that are measured for or by the client, as discussed in the previous chapter.

When

- Although the client may assess compliance with the SLA or contract as little as once a year, the provider will need to monitor this aspect of its performance much more frequently, say monthly. Of course, serious service problems have to be dealt with as they arise.

Customer satisfaction and client engagement

What

- The provider needs to know how satisfied its clients and users are with the service and to understand areas of contentment and concern. Typically, as discussed in the previous chapter, it could use a survey with a five-point scale of: very satisfied, satisfied, neither satisfied nor dissatisfied, dissatisfied and very dissatisfied, supplemented by open questions on what is good and what needs to improve.
- The provider will engage with the client's management and users as a matter of course, e.g. through project and service desk contact.

For an effective relationship, it is also important that there is systematic senior management contact between the two sides, to discuss the state of the service and the relationship, as well as plans and strategic direction. So the provider may want to keep count of how often these contacts take place.

When

- An annual customer satisfaction survey should be enough for a provider that systematically engages with clients, but the frequency may need to be increased if the service becomes unstable, or if there are grounds for thinking that customer satisfaction is suboptimal.
- Depending on how vital IT is for the business and the extent to which business transformation needs to be IT-driven, senior contacts should take place up to several times a year and stock should be taken of these contacts at least once a year.

Costs and charges: value for money

What

- The provider will want to keep the costs that it incurs to a minimum, consistent with providing an effective service to its clients and with sustaining long-term relationships with them. By keeping the lid on costs, the provider helps contain the charges it needs to levy on clients, thus maintaining competitiveness and sustaining profitability. So the provider needs to keep measuring its costs, to keep them under control.

- For service operations, a headline measure of the cost per user gives a helpful indication of cost efficiency. Cost per user would be assessed as: (total cost of live operation) ÷ (number of users). If need be, the headline figure can be supplemented by more specific information on components of the service provision, such as the cost of the service desk.

- For projects and smaller-scale changes, the cost to the provider per project and per change should be accounted for, which will involve measurement, in some form, of staff deployment. A more detailed breakdown of costs per project phase may be needed, with reasons for any deviation from the project's planned costs, to keep project costs under control.

- The provider should understand the cost of dealing with incidents and problems. Even for the best-run services, some incidents and problems are inevitable, but providers will want to minimise their problems, prevent incident recurrence and contain costs associated with the incidents and problems that do occur. To understand what is going on, the provider will need to have a breakdown by problem category, such as capacity, configuration.

When

- The finance department will normally lay down the timing of cost monitoring, which may well be monitored against budget every month.

- Cost per user should be gauged regularly, say once a quarter, to ensure the provider is well placed to contain costs and present itself in the best possible light to the client.

- Project and change costs need to be monitored against plans (budgets) in-flight, with regular reviews to take stock, say monthly to quarterly depending on circumstances.

- Where the costs of handling incidents and problems warrants it, they should be regularly tracked and reviewed, say monthly to quarterly as for changes. If these costs are assessed per category, e.g. hardware fault, software release fault, it will help the provider understand where to concentrate efforts to stabilise the system.

Availability and other service problems

What

- The provider needs to measure the availability of the infrastructure and key applications. Where several locations are served, it may be necessary to break the figures down by location. The basic statistic for availability is percentage uptime per period, but to get an assessment of service reliability, providers also need mean time between faults. From a problem management perspective, mean time to resolve is also important.

- The provider needs statistics on service problems, including those that fall short of non-availability. It is helpful to have frequency and duration statistics both on incidents, which are service disruptions, and on problems, their underlying cause. An incident can be addressed by providing a workaround, whereas the underlying problem needs to be resolved to provide a proper solution and prevent a recurrence of the incident. IT providers normally classify incidents and problems by severity and have different time-to-resolve targets for each severity level; the incident resolution targets are likely to be included in client SLAs. It is helpful to break the statistics down by incident/problem category, e.g. hardware fault, release fault, capacity shortfall.

When

- Statistics should be collected regularly, say monthly, to help the provider manage down problems. See the '*Measures for the business: checklist*' in *Chapter 5* for a discussion on measurement periods. Service incidents and problems do, of course, need to be managed in-flight.

Projects

What

- Important end-project measures include cost versus budget (see above), time versus plan, and an assessment of the delivery to requirement. The incidence and significance of project changes, issues and problems should be tracked to facilitate the management of the project in hand and to help iron out the client's and provider's approach for the benefit of future projects.

- Some form of post-project assessment of the quality of the project's delivery to the live service is needed to help ensure issues, both with the delivery in question and with the approach to projects more generally, can be tackled.

When

- The end-project measures need to be tracked and managed during the execution of each project. The end-project statistics also need to be regularly reviewed across the range of projects, the frequency depending on the organisation's project load, say annually for an organisation running one or two projects and quarterly for one running several projects a year.
- A post-project assessment is usually carried out two or three months after delivery. Stock should be taken of post-project assessments across the range of projects, to the same frequency as the end-project statistics above.

Service changes

What

- Changes to IT services can range from the introduction of major new applications delivered by projects, to enable client-led business change, through the introduction of significant software or hardware updates, typically provider- or supplier-led, to smallish-scale application changes at user request. See '*Projects*' (above) and '*Transition management*' (below) for coverage specific to projects and significant updates.

- The provider needs to understand the incidence of changes and their source (e.g. authorised project, supplier software update, client request), their cost (see '*Costs and charges: value for money*' above) and, through the problem management system, whether their introduction leads to service faults or instability.

When

- A regular review of planned changes and statistics on actual changes will show whether corrective action is needed to processes or software/hardware. Frequency could be quarterly to monthly, depending on the level of change being handled and whether there are any concerns about it.

Business continuity

What

- Both the provider and its clients will need to have a means of sustaining at least the most vital services, should some calamity affect staff, premises, the IT itself or the environment. The client and the provider should both, therefore, have business continuity plans, approved by their respective senior management and tested. The provider's business continuity plan should include a client-oriented IT continuity plan supporting the client's business continuity plan. There should be a clear, agreed definition of what constitutes a business continuity incident (an event triggering the deployment of either organisation's business continuity plan), so that statistics on the number and seriousness of such incidents can be tracked and lessons learned.

When

- An annual review should be carried out of the existence, testing and currency of the business continuity plan and of the statistics on business continuity incidents. The frequency should be increased if the circumstances require it.

Infrastructure and applications

What

- The provider needs to be on top of its hardware and software assets. All assets should be reviewed from time to time to check if they are still needed, up to date (current from the provider's perspective), known to the provider (they have not been obtained 'under the radar') and licensed. Statistics should be maintained on problems affecting hardware and software, to enable weak spots to be identified and corrective action to be taken.

6: What IT providers need to measure

When

- As a minimum, an inventory review should be carried out once a year. Hardware and software stability should be assessed in line with problem management systems, typically once a month (see above).

Suppliers

What

- The provider needs to track its own suppliers' performance and will have a particular interest in adherence to contract, prices/value-for-money, problem statistics and its own staff's customer satisfaction with suppliers.

When

- Supplier management statistics should be assembled regularly, e.g. quarterly or monthly and to align with liaison meetings. Satisfaction with suppliers should be assessed at least once a year.

Transition management

What

- From time to time, providers introduce new software or hardware, whether to cater for a new version of an operating system, to upgrade the client staff's laptops, to introduce an improved version of an application system, or for some other reason. The provider needs statistics to indicate how well these new releases are planned, communicated/consulted on, tested and rolled out, and how well they perform in practice. The required statistics should show up in service transition incidents through the problem management system (except performance in practice, which will be manifest in service operation incidents).

When

- As ever, incidents need to be managed in-flight. Statistics on transition incidents need to be reviewed for lessons learned post-transition, say from one to three months after the new release goes live. Problem management statistics should be reviewed for release-related problems in the operational system, at the same time.

Technology

What

- The provider and, in many cases, the client will want reassurance that the provider's approach to technology change is strategically acceptable; as an example, this may mean not being too leading edge on things like operating systems but taking full advantage of things like the Cloud. There are no magic measurements for this, but the provider should ask itself the question regularly, with clients where appropriate, of whether it is as up to date with technology as it needs to be.

When

- Some form of annual technology review would be prudent.

CHAPTER 7: PROCESS MEASURES

Knowing how things work is the basis for appreciation and is thus a source of civilised delight. William Safire

In this chapter, we consider the measurement of IT provider processes, as a basis for more deeply understanding IT provision and improving it.

Any business organisation works by taking inputs and subjecting them to a transformation process to create outputs. If the process, at macro level, is IT provision, the organisation's users will be interested in some or all of the inputs and outputs, but that is normally as far and as deep as their interest in the processes will go. By analogy, if you go to see a film, you'll be interested in the inputs that you yourself provide (how much you pay) and in how the outputs affect you personally, for example, whether it's enjoyable or stimulating and whether the seats are comfortable. It's unlikely you'll be interested in the processes involved in providing the film, whether that is in its making, its distribution or in its showing at the cinema.

As we have been seeing, IT providers need to be very interested in their inputs and outputs (and often outcomes), as seen from both their customers' and their own perspectives. To make sure they deliver what is needed, effectively and efficiently, they need to be on top of their own processes.

To take an example of project management, the provider will want to be satisfied that its track record on projects shows delivery to time, to budget and to specification – and really to customer satisfaction. If not, it will want to delve deeper to find out why and who isn't doing what right, so that things can be put right. It may even be that either the provider or the client organisation doesn't have a mature, repeatable project process, so what happens is completely down to the experience or otherwise of individuals. It may also be that the project personnel are not trained or capable. These problems would show up on an assessment (e.g. a capability maturity assessment) of the project process. There could be shortfalls in the way project costs are managed or a failure to control scope or manage change. Diagnostic information on these problems would be obtainable by assessing project sub-processes to do with cost and change management.

Moving on from projects to operational IT, the current version of ITIL refers to a set of service management processes, categorised by phases in the service management life cycle. It is beyond the scope of this book to suggest measurements for each of these processes, but the following discussion gives a flavour of the issues in play and the decisions to be made.

Bear in mind, too, that if you measure compliance with processes or procedures, it has to be with these as defined in your organisation. You aren't in a position to measure compliance with a framework like ITIL because frameworks aren't generally defined tightly enough to allow it.

Providers will need to make sure they get enough information to make informed decisions. There is a big risk of over-measuring and over-analysing. As it says elsewhere in this book, don't spend more on measurement than you gain through the actions you take as a response to the measurements!

Here are key questions the provider needs to answer about its processes:

- Do my processes contribute to fulfilment of my obligations to client organisations?
- Do they work effectively and efficiently, judging by quality and consistency of results and by input resources?
- Are the processes well defined and repeatable?
- Are the processes resourced by competent personnel and led by competent leaders?
- Do the processes work seamlessly and effectively with each other?
- Are the teams that depend on the processes satisfied with their quality and effectiveness?

Let us consider capacity management. The discussion below refers to ITIL v3 and its updated form ITIL 2011.

The *ITIL Service Design* book[1] refers to various capacity management objectives, some of which have associated deliverables, such as an up-to-date capacity plan reflecting current and future business needs.

---

[1] Office of Government Commerce (OGC) (2007), *ITIL Service Design*, TSO (now superseded by the 2011 edition, authored by the Cabinet Office and also published by the TSO).

The existence of the capacity plan can be checked. So can the incidence and seriousness of problems to the provider and its customers stemming from any inadequacies in the capacity plan. For example, when projects deliver new functionality, the provider needs there to be enough of the right capacity to allow the new facility to run effectively. Just think of the number of times a new service gets launched and the website crashes! This might be a problem caused by the failure of capacity management to plan enough capacity or to control launch-day demand.

Is capacity management contributing to fulfilment of provider obligations to clients?

Viewed from the perspective of what is getting in the way of fulfilling contractual or SLA commitments to client organisations, statistics on incidents and problems can tell the provider a lot about processes that should have prevented the problem in the first place. Processes to assess by means of incident and problem statistics include: availability, capacity, information security, and release and supplier management.

Judging by inputs and results, is capacity management efficient and effective?

If the evidence shows that customer commitments are not being jeopardised by capacity management problems, to that extent the process is effective. It might still not be effective or efficient from the provider's perspective though; other provider teams may be having to cover up or compensate by doing more work themselves. Issues will show up in problem statistics and in provider teams' satisfaction with capacity management. If the statistics are spiky, they will need to be looked at to check whether there's a reasonable explanation for the spikes, or whether it's a matter of capacity management performance being erratic.

At the same time, the provider will want to be satisfied that capacity management is efficient: 'are we getting our money's worth'? There are no absolute measures that can be used to check, but comparisons with other IT providers' capacity management team costs, and with its own over a period, will provide some indication.

Are the processes well defined and repeatable?

It almost goes without saying that well-defined, documented processes to which staff comply are more efficient than a make-it-up-as-you-go approach. Moreover, a well-defined process provides a much better basis for improvement than something ill-defined and ad hoc.

There is no magic measurement; either the processes are documented or they are not. An assessment of staff's compliance can be carried out by an independent external or internal inspection, or as part of a formal certification to ISO9000[2], which then is refreshed from time to time.

---

[2] ISO 9000, *Quality management systems*, Geneva: International Organization for Standardization (ISO).

Are the processes resourced and led by competent personnel?

IT providers can lay down the competency levels they require of IT leaders and staff and can stipulate specific expertise in processes, such as capacity management. It is then a matter of assessing staff's suitability against the requirements and either allocating qualified staff, or developing people on the job to get them to the required level.

Are provider processes working seamlessly together?

Capacity management, as we are seeing, needs to work with various IT provision processes. Problem statistics and internal satisfaction with capacity management will reveal how well that seamlessness is working in practice.

One important aspect of seamlessness is the synergy created out of what could easily become conflicting processes. The quick resolution of incidents at the expense of fixing underlying problems is a *cause célèbre* illustrating the need for proper synergy between incident and problem management. A process that could easily get into conflict with capacity management is availability management, with the latter quite likely to press for some duplicate capacity to provide resilience and the former equally likely to say it's excessive. It will be up to the provider's leadership to manage these conflicts, driven by the right balance of customer needs and provider costs. Statistics on internal satisfaction among provider teams will generally show where there are threats to seamlessness.

Are the teams that rely on capacity management satisfied?

An assessment of the satisfaction of teams that rely on capacity management can be tailored to 'what good looks like'. As an illustration, team satisfaction could be assessed against the following expectations:

- service operations: IT providers would expect to be satisfied that service quality is not jeopardised by capacity problems (in other words, poor capacity management);
- projects: project teams should be able to rely on capacity management to handle capacity planning for projects' outputs;
- service transition: service transition should be free of capacity problems, as new or changed facilities are released onto the IT service.

CHAPTER 8: ONWARDS AND UPWARDS

Never rest on your laurels.

Not done yet

In this book, we've focused on the measurement of IT provision from both customer and provider perspectives.

Enlightened IT providers will have a disciplined approach to their work, often based on IT industry standards and leading frameworks such as ITIL. Enlightened clients may well demand that their provider use standardised approaches – or proof that the provider's approaches are to an equivalent high standard.

The use of a disciplined approach makes it easier to use measurement as a basis for improvement, in the same way that it's easier to measure an engineer's work and use the measurement for improvement, than it is to do that with an artist's work.

If you need to improve your IT provision, you should consider using industry-leading frameworks and measurement associated with the frameworks, to raise your game.

If you think there's a bewildering array of IT management frameworks that overlap and leave gaps, consider the following. The leading frameworks between them cover most of the ground associated with IT provision. So you can use things like:

- the Balanced Scorecard approach to improve strategic management of the business (and IT as a business in its own right);
- Lean and SixSigma to improve business processes;
- ISO9000 and capability maturity model integration (CMMI®) to help ensure you have a disciplined approach to quality management and IT provision respectively;
- Managing Successful Programmes (MSP®), Project Management Body of Knowledge (PMBOK®) and/or PRINCE2 to manage programmes and projects;
- COBIT® to foster good governance;
- Application Services Library (ASL®) to manage application software; and
- ITIL for IT service management.

When to use each of these, and how to deploy measurement based on them, would fill at least one book in its own right. So: use the Web; do your research, talk to others and make choices relevant to your situation and the imperatives faced by your organisation.

Conclusion

IT is a service to businesses and often a business in its own right. It exists in a dynamic environment, with technology advances being made all the time. These advances enable businesses to do new things and to do existing things better: to be more customer-friendly and more efficient. IT operations are highly visible to customers, whose lives and work in all likelihood depend on it.

8: Onwards and upwards

IT expenditure is a sizeable chunk of most organisations' spend. IT's contribution is typically much more significant than the amount spent on it.

Being an IT provider is an important, challenging role. Being a client is the same.

Being a good provider or a good client demands understanding and continual attention – sometimes likened to running to stand still. You can only do it effectively with measurement.

Measurement is a means to the end of satisfied IT customers, provided with a good IT service that meets their needs now and in the future, and that represents value for money.

If you're an IT provider, measuring yourself this year against last year should show an improvement in satisfaction, service quality, process quality and value for money. There are two exceptions: if you were perfect already or if you have experienced significant change. If you aren't improving year-on-year, you need to understand why and may need to take action.

If you're a business that uses IT, your provider should be giving you better satisfaction, better service and better value for money this year compared with last: unless, of course, you were completely satisfied last year that your service was already excellent in terms of quality and value for money. Equally, you can't expect everything to keep getting better in times of hefty change.

It isn't enough just to improve; providers need to be a match for competitors. They can compare themselves with others, through measurement or benchmarking communities.

8: Onwards and upwards

Power to those who measure up and improve!

Postscript

Whether you see IT as a business enabler or as a necessary evil will depend on your perspective, your job and your experience. If it allows your business to revolutionise itself or to attract a lot of new customers, you'll look on it positively. If you're a sole trader who has lost data and had to rebuild your system twice this year, you may not be so well disposed.

We've been exploring how to measure IT to check it does what it says on the tin, without having to spend too much.

Be careful, though, not to use measurement to optimise the wrong thing. 'Doing IT right' is, of course, what everybody wants, but 'doing the right things with IT' is why the business invests in it in the first place. So don't forget to check the business value of IT. If you're lucky, your organisation will have a business case justifying the expenditure on IT and setting out the value the business expects to get from it. The benefits can't always be measured, but it's important nevertheless to check they're being achieved, month by month, year by year. Don't make your IT efficient or economic by putting its effective support to the business in jeopardy.

ITG RESOURCES

IT Governance Ltd. sources, creates and delivers products and services to meet the real-world, evolving IT governance needs of today's organisations, directors, managers and practitioners.

The ITG website (_www.itgovernance.co.uk_) is the international one-stop-shop for corporate and IT governance information, advice, guidance, books, tools, training and consultancy.

Other Websites

Books and tools published by IT Governance Publishing (ITGP) are available from all business booksellers and are also immediately available from the following websites:

http://www.itgovernance.eu is our euro-denominated website which ships from Benelux and has a growing range of books in European languages other than English.

www.itgovernanceusa.com is a US$-based website that delivers the full range of IT Governance products to North America, and ships from within the continental US.

www.itgovernanceasia.com provides a selected range of ITGP products specifically for customers in the Indian subcontinent.

www.itgovernance.asia delivers the full range of ITGP publications, serving countries across Asia-Pacific. Shipping from Hong Kong, US dollars, Singapore dollars, Hong Kong dollars, New Zealand dollars and Thai baht are all accepted through the website.

www.27001.com is the IT Governance Ltd. website that deals specifically with information security management, and ships from within the continental US.

Toolkits

ITG's unique range of toolkits includes the IT Governance Framework Toolkit, which contains all the tools and guidance that you will need in order to develop and implement an appropriate IT governance framework for your organisation. Full details can be found at *www.itgovernance.co.uk/ products/519*.

For a free paper on how to use the proprietary Calder-Moir IT Governance Framework, and for a free trial version of the toolkit, see *www.itgovernance.co.uk/calder_moir.aspx*.

There is also a wide range of toolkits to simplify implementation of management systems, such as an ISO/IEC 27001 ISMS or an ISO/IEC 22301 BCMS, and these can all be viewed and purchased online at: *http://www.itgovernance.co.uk/catalog/1*.

Training Services

IT Governance offers an extensive portfolio of training courses designed to educate information security, IT governance, risk management and compliance professionals. Our classroom and online training programmes will help you develop the skills required to deliver best practice and compliance to your organisation. They will also enhance your career by providing you with industry standard certifications and increased peer recognition. Our range of courses offer a structured learning path from foundation to advanced level in the key topics of information security, IT governance, business continuity and service management.

ISO/IEC 20000 is the first international standard for IT service management and has been developed to reflect the best practice guidance contained within the ITIL framework. Our ISO20000 Foundation and Practitioner training courses are designed to provide delegates with a comprehensive introduction and guide to the implementation of an ISO20000 management system and an industry-recognised qualification awarded by APMG International.

Full details of all IT Governance training courses can be found at *http://www.itgovernance.co.uk/ training.aspx*

Professional Services and Consultancy

IT Governance consultants have the expertise to help you understand, control or improve your IT and, just as importantly, communicate measurement results effectively to stakeholders.

We can show you how good your IT is, both in terms of quality and value for money, through the use of effective measurement techniques. Then you will understand whether you can keep what you have as it is, or if you need to make improvements to your system on the basis of evidence in the form of accurate data.

We have substantial real-world experience as a professional services company specialising in IT GRC-related management systems, so applying metrics through the Plan, Do, Check, Act cycle is integral to our work. In the same way, we can assist you in the design and deployment of IT service management structures, such as ITIL and ISO20000, and integrate them with other systems' approaches such as ISO27001, ISO22301, ISO14001 and COBIT® – supporting and enabling measurable improvements in the effectiveness of your business processes.

For more information about IT Governance consultancy to improve measurement techniques and supply accurate data, visit our site: *http://www.itgovernance.co.uk/consulting.aspx.*

Publishing Services

IT Governance Publishing (ITGP) is the world's leading IT GRC publishing imprint that is wholly owned by IT Governance Ltd.

With books and tools covering all IT governance, risk and compliance frameworks, we are the publisher of choice for authors and distributors alike, producing unique and practical publications of the highest quality, in the latest formats available, which readers will find invaluable.

www.itgovernancepublishing.co.uk is the website dedicated to ITGP, enabling both current and future authors, distributors, readers and other interested parties to have easier access to more information, allowing them to keep up to date with the latest publications and news from ITGP.

Newsletter

IT governance is one of the hottest topics in business today, not least because it is also the fastest moving.

You can stay up to date with the latest developments across the whole spectrum of IT governance subject matter, including risk management, information security, ITIL and IT service management, project governance, compliance and so much more, by

subscribing to ITG's core publications and topic alert emails.

Simply visit our subscription centre and select your preferences:
www.itgovernance.co.uk/newsletter.aspx.